GREATER THINGS

Qualifications of a Biblical Leader

PAUL SWAMIDASS

VIDE

Vide Press
6200 Second Street
Washington D.C. 20011
www.VidePress.com

ISBN 978-1-7351814-7-9

Printed in the United States of America

To my parents and grandparents for
generational faith and blessings.

Jesus on "Greater things"

Then Nathanael declared, "Rabbi, you are the Son of God; you are the king of Israel." Jesus said, "You believe because I told you I saw you under the fig tree. You will see greater things than that." (John 1:50)

Preface

This book is a bird's eye view of the qualifications of a Biblical leader, entirely based on the Bible. One would be surprised at the extent of material the Bible contains on the qualifications of a Biblical leader, which should be the norm for Christian leaders today; the terms "Biblical leader" and "Christian leader" are used interchangeably in the book.

An investigation of the qualifications of a Biblical leader is recommended for those preparing to be Christian leaders as well as those who are seasoned leaders. This book can serve as a tool to perform self-examination by future and current leaders to grasp what the Bible expects from them as Biblical leaders.

The topics covered in this book could be introduced at the start a Christian leadership training session before getting into the nuts and bolts of leadership training. Numerous books on the nuts and bolts of Christian leadership are in the market. Such books can be considered appropriate companion material for this book.

This book offers new and fresh perspectives on trying leadership situations and experiences of leaders in the Bible. Each chapter addresses a single leadership principle, therefore you may read the chapters in any order you wish.

The expectations, vision, and purpose of Biblical leaders are different from those of successful worldly leaders. Some key aspects of Christian leadership do not apply to secular, worldly leaders; **if you wonder what they are, this book is for you!**

The qualities that make a Biblical leader distinct from secular leaders can be found in Jesus, Moses, David, the Apostle Paul, and many others including lesser known common folks from the Bible. Their lives, their teachings, and their actions that are fit for leaders are scrutinized carefully to draw lessons on Biblical leadership in this book; each chapter is focused on a single lesson.

To be a Christian leader, it is **not enough** to know the leadership principles that are proven successful in the secular world or the leadership principles taught in a business school. The Apostle Paul's vision explained by him to King Agrippa in Acts 26 and Moses' call to lead at the "bush" described in Exodus 3 are unique to Biblical leaders. Jesus also expects leaders to practice justice, mercy, and faithfulness toward those they lead (Matthew 23). Furthermore, in the actions and lives of Moses, Paul, David, Solomon, Aaron, and others, we see the right things to do or the things to avoid as Biblical leaders.

Jesus exemplifies leadership. He offered Himself as an example when He taught the disciples about servant leadership. In the events from the Bible included here, Jesus teaches and admonishes leaders for their shortcomings; we can learn from both.

There are many examples of good leaders as well as failed leaders in the Bible. We can learn from both; that is the premise of this book.

The chapters are presented in a short format for use with or without a teacher. The chapters can be used in group discussions, too.

Leading questions are included at the end of each chapter. During self-study, the questions provide a sense of direction to the study, whether one is a beginner or a seasoned leader. Additionally, the questions at the end of each chapter are meant to enhance learning from the chapter. The questions could also serve as a useful tool during chapter-by-chapter group discussion.

Motivated leaders subject themselves to leadership development all their lives. Rob McKenna, in his blog *The Leader Development Crisis* for Christian Leadership Alliance (May 18, 2020), said this: "Leaders develop in situations where they are pushed to the edge of themselves … and in situations where they are asked to lead at levels of scope they have never experienced before." We find excellent teachable examples of these very situations and experiences in the Bible.

This compact book of twenty-four chapters is the first volume in the planned series on Biblical leadership. After reading this book, I hope you would agree with me that the Bible is an endless storage of lessons for Christian leaders, who are on the journey to see (John 1:50) and do "greater things" (John 14:12). Jesus called ordinary men as His disciples to see and do "greater things."

[Note: The New International Version (niv) is used throughout the book except one instance in Chapter 19, in which the use of the English Standard Version (esv) is identified.]

Paul Swamidass
Auburn, Alabama, USA
2020

Table of Contents

SECTION I

Vision, Priorities, and Victories

Lesson

LESSON 1

A Vision of Greater Things

One of the most exhilarating moments recorded in the gospels occurred when Nathaniel met Jesus Christ. He exclaimed: *"Rabbi, you are the Son of God; You are the King of Israel!"* (John 1:49). Jesus' response was timeless: *"You will see greater things than that"* (John 1:50).

In American slang, for emphasis, Jesus might have sounded like this: "You ain't seen nothin' yet!"

"You will see greater things" is an exalted summary of a vision statement. Any vision statement that merits this description will never become stale and will always point to "greater things" in the future. Jesus' promise, "You will see greater things," can guide the formulation of vision statements for Christian leaders as well as Christian organizations.

What did Jesus mean by "greater things"? Did Jesus refer to His own many miracles or His disciples' miracles, His teachings, His arrest and crucifixion, His resurrection, His ascension, the outpouring of the Holy Spirit upon His followers in Jerusalem, the bold witness of His disciples in Jerusalem and outside Jerusalem, the martyrdom of Jesus' disciples, the explosive growth of the church under the leadership of His disciples both in Jerusalem and in faraway places among Gentiles, or something more?

A Vision of the Future for Peter

After His resurrection, Jesus asked Peter three times, "Do you love me?" Peter was disappointed that Jesus asked him the same question three times.

3

Peter was hurt because Jesus asked him the third time, "Do you love me?" He said, "Lord, you know all things; you know that I love you."

Jesus said, "Feed my sheep." (John 21:17)

Each time Peter assured Jesus that he loved him, Jesus responded to Peter saying one of the following: *"Feed my lambs ... take care of my sheep ... feed my sheep"* (John 21:15–17). Collectively, this is a vision of "greater things" that Jesus wanted Peter to "see." But, based on Peter's responses to Jesus that day, he did not get the vision, although, Jesus said it three times, and in three different ways for emphasis. This illustrates how we may miss it, when Jesus shows us greater things.

However, later, in Acts 4, we see Peter gets it. It is recorded,

The priests and the captain of the temple guard and the Sadducees came up to Peter and John while they were speaking to the people. They were greatly disturbed because the apostles were teaching the people, proclaiming in Jesus the resurrection of the dead. They seized Peter and John and, because it was evening, they put them in jail until the next day. But many who heard the message believed; so the number of men who believed grew to about five thousand. (Acts 4:1–4)

This was merely one example of the "greater things" Peter would see again and again. But that was not all.

Troubled by the massive public response to Peter and John, the high priest and other leaders said to themselves,

"We must warn them to speak no longer to anyone in this name."

Then they called them in again and commanded them not to speak or teach at all in the name of Jesus. But Peter and John replied, "Which is right in God's eyes: to listen to you, or to

him? You be the judges! As for us, we cannot help speaking about what we have seen and heard."

After further threats they let them go. They could not decide how to punish them, because all the people were praising God for what had happened. For the man who was miraculously healed was over forty years old. (Acts 4:17–22)

Both Peter and John resisted; no earthly authority was going to stop them from pursuing their bright and beautiful vision of "greater things."

Yes, Peter was not going to stopped from "feeding the sheep," just as Jesus told him to do, not long ago.

Discuss from a Christian Leader's Perspective:

1. What does "You will see greater things" mean to you?

2. As a Christian leader, are you seeing "greater things"? If not, why not?

Apostle Paul: Obey Your Vision

"So then, King Agrippa, I was not disobedient to the vision from heaven." (Acts 26:19)

Have you ever wondered what Apostle Paul meant by this?

Paul, an Unusual Prisoner

Festus, the incoming Roman governor at Caesarea, inherited an unusual prisoner from Felix, the outgoing governor. The unusual prisoner was Paul the Apostle, who was imprisoned unjustly at Caesarea for two years (Acts 24:27).

As Festus took over, Jewish leaders in Jerusalem asked him to send Paul to Jerusalem to be tried by them. Paul, to avoid a trial at Jerusalem by angry Jews, who caused his arrest, formally appealed to Caesar (per Roman law). Because Festus granted Paul's appeal to be heard by Caesar at Rome (Acts 25:12), he avoided the trial at Jerusalem, but was made to wait in the prison until the trip to Rome materialized.

Not long after Festus assumed his role as the local governor, King Agrippa paid him a surprise visit.

Paul's case was so perplexing to Festus that he chose to take advantage of the king's visit to ask his help in resolving his concerns about Paul, the unusual prisoner. Festus acknowledged that Paul had no charges worthy of imprisonment, much less a trip to Rome for a hearing before Caesar.

This is what Festus confessed to visiting King Agrippa about Apostle Paul:

> But I have nothing definite to write to His Majesty [Roman Caesar] about him. Therefore I have brought him before all of you, and especially before you, King Agrippa, so that as a result of this investigation I may have something to write. For I think it is unreasonable to send a prisoner on to Rome without specifying the charges against him. (Acts 25:26–27)

A Prisoner Not Focused on Complaints

At the formal hearing arranged for the king to hear Paul, who was in chains, Paul told King Agrippa about an incident two years earlier (Acts 21:31), when a commander of the local Roman troops saved him from a murderous mob of angry Jews at the Temple. After saving him from the mob, the commander chained and imprisoned Paul. This is how Paul summarized the event to the king:

> Some Jews [who were enraged by my teachings about Jesus Christ] seized me in the temple courts and tried to kill me. But God has helped me to this very day; so I stand here and testify to small and great alike. (Acts 26:21–22)

It is notable that Paul, chained and imprisoned for two years for no punishable crime, was mindful of God's help during his years of imprisonment. The king **did not hear from Paul any complaint against God or the Roman authorities for keeping him imprisoned, or complaints about mistreatments while in the Roman prison.** He did not complain or express anger/displeasure about unjust loss of freedom, either.

Instead, Paul described to the king his vision on the way to Damascus and **how he responded to his vision.**

> On one of these journeys I was going to Damascus with the authority and commission of the chief priests. About noon, King Agrippa, as I was on the road, I saw a light from heav-

en, brighter than the sun, blazing around me and my companions ... and I heard a voice saying to me in Aramaic ... "I am Jesus, whom you are persecuting." (Acts 26:12–15)

Paul Described His Vision

Without taking time to voice any complaints to the king, Paul described his vision to the king and his resolve to be obedient to the vision at all costs. He quoted what Jesus said to him in his vision:

> *I have appeared to you to appoint you as a servant and as a witness of what you have seen and will see of me.... I am sending you to them [gentiles] to open their eyes and turn them from darkness to light, and from the power of Satan to God, so that they may receive forgiveness of sins and a place among those who are sanctified by faith in me.* (Acts 26:16–18)

Paul's vision would have been worthless if he disregarded it. Paul wanted to leave no doubt in the minds of all those, who heard him that day, how strongly that vision changed his life:

> *So then, King Agrippa, I was not disobedient to the vision from heaven. First to those in Damascus, then to those in Jerusalem and in all Judea, and then to the Gentiles, I preached that they should repent and turn to God and demonstrate their repentance by their deeds.* (Acts 26:19–20)

Paul's obedience to his vision was in full display even during the above audience with King Agrippa; Paul's life was laser-focused on persuading everyone to accept and follow Jesus Christ. None other than the king himself bears witness to Paul's single-minded pursuit of his vision:

> *Then Agrippa said to Paul, "Do you think that in such a short time you can persuade me to be a Christian?"*

Paul replied, "Short time or long—I pray to God that not only you but all who are listening to me today may become what I am, except for these chains." (Acts 26:28–29)

It appears that nothing can sway Paul from obeying his vision. Paul's words, his demeanor, and his attitude proclaim loudly and clearly, **"It is a privilege and honor for me to obey my vision, yesterday, today and tomorrow—it makes no difference whether I am a prisoner in chains or not. Further, it makes no difference to me whether my audience is made of royalty or not."**

I agree, it is rather uncommon to say, "Obey your vision," but it eloquently captures the meaning of what Apostle Paul said.

Discuss from a Christian Leader's Perspective:

1. How did Apostle Paul obey his vision?

2. Apostle Paul obeyed his vision. What about you?

3. Could you identify a few reasons why leaders may not obey their vision?

Apostle Paul: A Vision and an Action Plan

Every Call Deserves an Action Plan

In the epistle to the Romans (chapter 1:1–17), Apostle Paul described his calling as well as how he acted on his calling. For those who wonder what their own calling is, and how to translate their calling into action, Paul offers a powerful lesson from his own life.

His Calling and the Scope of His Call

> *Paul, a servant of Christ Jesus, called to be an apostle and set apart for the gospel of God ... regarding his son ... Jesus Christ our Lord.... Through him we received grace and apostleship to call all gentiles to obedience.* (Romans 1:1–5)

In these verses, we see three parts to his calling. First, he was called to be an apostle who was set apart for furthering the gospel. Given this challenging task, Paul acknowledged that he received God's grace to strengthen and embolden him to carry out his calling with divine wisdom. Finally, Paul defined the scope of his calling; "call ALL gentiles to obedience to the gospel," which covered the entire world. To summarize, Paul was called:

1. To be an apostle set apart for the gospel.

2. To receive God's grace to fulfill his calling.

3. To call ALL gentiles to obedience to the gospel.

Translating the Call to Action

To fulfill his call, Paul translated his call to a set of actions; read them in his own words in his letter to the Romans:

> *I long to see you so that I may impart to you* [Romans] *some spiritual gift to make you strong—that is, that you and I may be mutually encouraged by each other's faith. I planned many times to come to you … in order that I might have a harvest among you, just as I have had among the other Gentiles.*
>
> *I am obligated both to Greeks and non-Greeks, both to the wise and the foolish. That is why I am so eager to preach the gospel also to you who are in Rome.*
>
> *For I am not ashamed of the gospel…. "The righteous shall live by faith."* (Romans 1:11–17)

From these words of Apostle Paul addressed to the Roman Christians, we can infer the following list of things formed his action plan to fulfill his calling:

1. Sought the opportunity to impart some spiritual gifts to Roman believers to make them strong and to mutually encourage each other's faith (vv. 11–12).

2. Sought a harvest among Romans (v. 13).

3. Was obligated to give the gospel to people of all description, including Greeks, etc. (v. 14).

4. Was eager to preach the gospel in Rome (v. 15).

5. Was not ashamed of the gospel (v. 16)—a prerequisite to carry out his calling.

6. Lived by faith (v. 17)—a prerequisite for success.

Note that Paul mentions two essential prerequisites that ensured the success of his calling. First, he lived by faith in God (item 6), which formed the foundation for his work. Second, to preach the gospel effectively to all, he was proud of it, or in other words, he was not ashamed of it (item 5). Without these two prerequisites, his calling would have come to a screeching halt.

Remember, Paul was not ignoring existing Roman believers while seeking to give the gospel to nonbelievers in Rome; he wanted to impart spiritual gifts to Roman believers so that he and the local believers could be mutually encouraged by each other's faith (item 1).

Paul's Ministry beyond the Grave

Paul aggressively preached and taught the gospel through face-to-face encounters as well as through the vehicle of his letters to remote churches. Further, through his epistles, for more than 2,000 years, Paul continued to preach and teach the gospel to ALL people around the world since he went home.

Therefore, while Paul may be dead, because of his epistles, his ministry is undying.

We all can rejoice and say the Apostle Paul was obedient to his calling to reach ALL gentiles, both during and after his life on Earth! He is a great role model for leaders.

Discuss from a Christian Leader's Perspective:

1. What do you learn from Paul's action plan?

2. What is your action plan to implement God's call?

3. How could you improve your action plan to better implement God's call based on your past successes and failures, and based on the Apostle Paul's action plan?

Driven by Your Top Priority

Jesus Spells Out the Priority for Us

Our top priority ought to drive us. Jesus noticed a problem with the priorities of His followers. Jesus noticed that their top priority was being eroded by mundane problems and worries. Jesus prescribed their top priority this way:

> *So do not worry, saying, "What shall we eat?" or "What shall we drink?" or "What shall we wear?" ...* **But seek first his kingdom and his righteousness,** *and all these things will be given to you as well.* (Matthew 6:31–33)

What are a leader's priorities? They are found in the ordering of a leader's objectives. Priorities acknowledge that:

1. All objectives are not equally important,

2. Higher ranked objectives are more important than lower ranked objectives, and

3. One objective tops the list, and it should never be compromised.

Concerning priorities, we can learn much from two leaders who are described at length in the Bible: King Solomon and the Apostle Paul.

King Solomon Had Everything

King Solomon accomplished many earthly goals, perhaps more than any other ruler, man or woman. He also had great skills. Here are some of his tangible accomplishments that are recorded (1 Kings 9:15–26):

1. Built the Lord's temple and his own palace (v. 15),

2. Constructed the terraces and the wall of Jerusalem (v. 15),

3. Built Hazor, Megiddo, and Gezer (v. 15),

4. Rebuilt Gezer and Lower Beth Horon (v. 17),

5. Built Baalath, Tadmor in the desert, and all his store cities and the towns for his chariots and horses—and whatever he desired to build in Jerusalem, in Lebanon, and throughout all the territory he ruled (v. 18–19).

6. Built ships at Ezion (v. 26).

In addition, for a good measure, the Bible says that King Solomon had wisdom, knowledge, wealth, and an abundance of possessions (2 Chronicles 1:12).

Solomon Lost His Priority

When he lost track of his priorities sometime during his royal life, King Solomon angered God and learned the hard way to get his priorities right toward the end of his life.

When Solomon lost track of his priorities, the Bible says,

> The LORD became angry with Solomon because his heart had turned away from the LORD, the God of Israel, who had appeared to him twice. Although he had forbidden Solomon to follow other gods, Solomon did not keep the LORD's command. (1 Kings 11:9–10)

King Solomon made two statements about his priorities that reveal what he learned about priorities.

First, in Ecclesiastes, he declared everything and every accomplishment was "meaningless" or "vanity." He said:

The words of the Teacher, son of David, king in Jerusalem: "Meaningless! Meaningless!" says the Teacher. "Utterly meaningless! Everything is meaningless." What do people gain from all their labors at which they toil under the sun? (Ecclesiastes 1:1–3)

Regains His Priority

The Lord's anger appears to have brought Solomon back, because near the end of his life, he makes a second statement about his priorities:

Now all has been heard; here is the conclusion of the matter: Fear God and keep his commandments, for this is the duty of all mankind. (Ecclesiastes 12:13)

By paraphrasing his two statements about priorities, we can state the king's complete statement of priorities towards the end of his life as this: **"Fear God and keep his commandments; everything else is vanity."**

What is notable about the king's statement is the fact he literally had "everything" before concluding "everything is vanity." His statement that "everything is vanity" is not a case of sour grapes.

King Solomon learned the hard way: "Fear God and keep his commandments; everything else is vanity." Solomon's decisions that led him astray teach us that leaders tend to lose track of their priorities by pursuing what he calls "vanities" or meaningless things of life.

Apostle Paul Had Very Little

The Apostle Paul makes this forceful statement to King Agrippa: *"So then, King Agrippa, I was not disobedient to the vision from heaven"* (Acts 26:19). This is only a partial statement of his priorities. Another part of his priorities is expressed in 1 Timothy 6:8, in which he said: *"But if we have food and clothing, we will be content with that."*

When we combine the two parts of Paul's priorities, we get this: **"To be totally obedient to God's vision, you need no more than food and clothing."**

It is notable that King Solomon (who had everything) and the Apostle Paul (who was reduced to food and clothing), both significant leaders in the Bible, living hundreds of years apart, agree with Jesus' teaching on priorities: "Seek first the Kingdom of God and his righteousness."

We learn from both leaders: Be driven by your top priority.

Discuss from a Christian Leader's Perspective:

1. Do you have a grasp of your top priority?

2. What are your main distractions from your top priority?

3. How do you handle distractions from your top priority?

SECTION II

Leadership Examples from the Bible

Lesson

LESSON 5

Moses: Unselfish leader

A Tragic Moment

There was a tragic moment when Moses was conversing with God on Mount Sinai (Exodus 32). Moses was unaware that his brother and partner, Aaron, was enabling the worship of a freshly cast golden calf at the foot of the mountain in defiance of God. God saw what transpired at the foot of the mountain, and He was angry.

God interrupted His conversation with Moses to say:

> "I have seen these people," the LORD said to Moses, "and they are a stiff-necked people. Now leave me alone so that my anger may burn against them and that I may destroy them. Then I will make you into a great nation." (Exodus 32:9–10)

Note the little-known but profound promise to Moses that God offers without Moses asking for it; it is the exact same promise God made to only one other person, Abraham in Genesis: "I will make you a great nation" (Genesis 12:2). Out of this promise to Abraham was born the nation of Israel.

Moses Defended the People

When God had decided to destroy the idol-worshipping nation of Israel at the foot of the mountain, Moses sensed a tragedy of immense proportions. As an unselfish leader and protector of those entrusted to him, he replied to God:

> "Why should your anger burn against your people, whom you brought out of Egypt with great power and a mighty

hand? Why should the Egyptians say, 'It was with evil intent that he brought them out, to kill them in the mountains and to wipe them off the face of the earth'? Turn from your fierce anger; relent and do not bring disaster on your people. Remember your servants Abraham, Isaac and Israel, to whom you swore by your own self: 'I will make your descendants as numerous as the stars in the sky and I will give your descendants all this land I promised them, and it will be their inheritance forever.'" Then the LORD relented and did not bring on his people the disaster he had threatened. (Exodus 32:11–14)

Moses' response reveals to me why God appeared to him at the "bush" and asked him to take the job of leading His people out of Egyptian slavery. During the bush encounter, God would not accept any of Moses' excuses for refusing his assignment.

Tragedy Averted by Moses

As an unselfish leader, Moses accomplished remarkable outcomes at this historic moment; they were:

1. He did not give up on the people he was leading. It is extremely significant that he did not say, "Yes, Lord. These unruly and difficult people are impossible to lead. They deserve anything and everything You want to throw at them. Give it to them!"

2. He unselfishly brushed aside God's promise to make him a great nation (the "nation of Moses," so to speak) at the expense of the nation of Israel. Note that Moses did not say, "Thank You for the promise to make me a great nation. After all that I did to confront the powerful Pharaoh in Egypt and to lead this unruly people out of Egypt, I deserve this honor as much as Abraham did."

3. His direct appeal to God for the welfare of the people helped change God's decision to destroy the nation of Israel ("The Lord relented," Exodus 32:14).

4. The tone of his above appeal to God shows assurance and a degree of boldness because it was a truly selfless appeal.

5. He was loyal to the people whose care was entrusted to him at the "bush."

6. Although, at the "bush," Moses was reluctant to take on the task of bringing the nation of Israel out of Egypt, once he took on the responsibility to be their leader, he unselfishly became their willing defender, protector, and savior.

A High Bar for Unselfish Leadership

Moses has set a very high bar for all leaders. Moses also demonstrated that unselfish leadership brings about remarkable outcomes; he was able to change God's decision and save lives.

As a mark of ultimate divine recognition of Moses, the Bible records that God attested to the fact that Moses was *"faithful in all my house"* (Numbers 12:7), implying he was the most faithful in God's sight. **His faithfulness to the people entrusted to his care was inseparable from his faithfulness to God.**

A call to "lead like Moses" is a tall order. Yet it is worth trying, with God's help.

Discuss from a Christian Leader's Perspective:

1. Why do you think Moses was so unselfish and he gave up so much?

2. What prepared Moses to be so unselfish?

3. Did God make the right choice by asking Moses at the "bush" to lead His people out of slavery?

4. Do you realize God must have prepared Moses for his role? Do you notice God preparing you?

Solomon: Wise Leader

A Challenge to the King's Wisdom

Wise decisions by leaders could be a blessing to all who are affected by such decisions as evidenced by the decisions of King Solomon. One of his famous decisions, as well as the process he used to arrive at that decision, is offered in the Bible as an example of Solomon's wisdom. This has stood the test of time as a sound example of wisdom for thousands of years.

The bizarre episode that set the stage for Solomon's famous wise decision concerned two quarrelling mothers. They appeared before King Solomon asking for a resolution of their dispute; each claimed a single baby as her own child. According to the Bible, this is how the episode reached a just and wise conclusion:

> *And so they* [the women] *argued before the king. The king said, "This one says, 'My son is alive and your son is dead,' while that one says, 'No! Your son is dead and mine is alive.'"*

> *Then the king said, "Bring me a sword." So they brought a sword for the king. He then gave an order: "Cut the living child in two and give half to one and half to the other."*

> *The woman whose son was alive was deeply moved out of love for her son and said to the king, "Please, my lord, give her the living baby! Don't kill him!"*

But the other said, "Neither I nor you shall have him. Cut him in two!"

Then the king gave his ruling: "Give the living baby to the first woman. Do not kill him; she is his mother." (1 Kings 3:23–27)

Wisdom Is Multi-Faceted

In this episode, as a leader, Solomon was faced with a tough decision. If he made an error, the child would end up with the wrong mother, and the real mother would be deprived of her child for life and would consequently grieve as long as she lived and would hate the king. What can leaders learn from Solomon's wise decision?

A dozen facets of this episode exemplify Solomon's wisdom:

1. Wisdom is wanting to do the right thing.

2. Wisdom is making the effort to find the truth.

3. Wisdom is treating with fairness both parties to the quarrel before the conflict is resolved.

4. Wisdom is diligently looking for truth hiding behind lies; liars can be as convincing as truth-tellers.

5. Wisdom is knowing how people would react to an unexpected surprise.

6. Wisdom is knowing how to surprise people to expose a lie.

7. Wisdom is knowing a real mother would save her baby's life, even if it means losing custody of her baby (the loving mother of Moses is evidence in Exodus 2:1–10).

8. Wisdom is knowing greed, selfishness, and raw envy may cause a person to take the life of another mother's innocent baby.

9. Wisdom is knowing a fake mother's love for a baby cannot match a real mother's love for her baby.

10. Wisdom is not favoring one side or the other in a conflict before successfully finding the underlying truth.

11. Wisdom is not using unsubstantiated shortcuts such as, "This mother looks more truthful to me, so I will decide in her favor," because appearances can be deceptive.

12. Wisdom is the ability to look beyond tears, as well as real or faked emotions of the parties to a conflict.

Learning from King Solomon

To make wise decisions, learn to incorporate appropriate facets of wisdom from the above list. For example, if **item 12** was the reason for one of your unwise decisions, ensure that you do not fall once again for real or fake emotions of parties to a conflict. If "unsubstantiated shortcut" (**item 11**) was the reason for one of your unwise decisions, remind yourself, "Looks can be deceptive," and therefore seek substantiating evidence before making a decision.

Above all, wisdom is **wanting to do the right thing (item 1)**. If this is not the driving force in a leader's decisions, wisdom will depart from the leader. Just as King Solomon faced a difficult decision, Aaron too faced a difficult decision when some men approached him, in the absence of Moses, asking for a golden calf to worship (Exodus 32:1–6). If he wanted to do the right thing, Aaron could have refused the request. But it appears that Aaron **did not even attempt to do the right thing** when he promptly enabled the mak-

31

ing and worshiping of a golden calf at the foot of Mount Sinai when Moses was away.

Aaron's unwise decision to enable the worship of a golden calf made God angry, and the consequences were severe: *"And the LORD struck the people with a plague because of what they did with the calf Aaron had made"* (Exodus 32:35). An unwise decision emerged when Aaron did not attempt to do the right thing (**item 1**).

Remember, King Solomon asked God, *"Give me wisdom and knowledge, that I may lead this people"* (2 Chronicles 1:10–12).

We know he received it generously. *"Blessed are those who find wisdom"* (Proverbs 3:13).

Discuss from a Christian Leader's Perspective:

1. What could you learn from Solomon's request to God, when he could have asked anything?

2. What facets of wisdom are unfamiliar to you, and how could you make them your own in future decisions?

3. To make wise decisions, what did you learn from Solomon?

Do the Right Thing

"Who Will Roll Away the Stone?"

When the Sabbath was over, Mary Magdalene, Mary the mother of James, and Salome bought spices so that they might go to anoint Jesus' body. Very early on the first day of the week, just after sunrise, they were on their way to the tomb and they asked each other, "Who will roll the stone away from the entrance of the tomb?" (Mark 16:1–3)

Jesus was crucified, dead, and buried before the event described in this passage. On the third day after the death of Jesus, out of their own initiative, the three women in this passage were driven to anoint and preserve with spices the lifeless body of Jesus inside the tomb.

They determined it was the right thing for them to do, no matter what. No one told them to do so.

It appears that they bought and prepared spices to anoint Jesus' body without first considering, "Who will roll away the massive stone blocking the entrance to his grave?" Or perhaps they did consider the challenge posed by the stone, but apparently they decided to prepare the spices first and to deal with the stone later, when they reach the tomb.

The women's family and friends may have reminded them, "You seem to be wasting your time and money on spices. Don't you know the tomb where Jesus' body lies is sealed by a large stone?"

Inaction Was Not an Option

The three women, with a common purpose, did NOT choose to wait around for the unlikely news, "The stone has been rolled away, and the tomb is now open and accessible." Waiting did not figure in their game plan.

You may wonder, "Why did they not seek the help of the disciples to roll the stone away?" The women did not verbalize their reason for ignoring the disciples, but their actions reveal their thinking, which may have sounded like this: "At this moment, having lost their leader, Jesus, the disciples are not ready, mentally or emotionally, for the task of rolling away the stone. So, let's leave them alone and take care of this in the best way we can." (Compare Mark 16:10.)

The women could have used the obstructing stone as a valid excuse for inaction, but they chose not to.

Surprised by the Rewarding Experience

On the first day of the week, once they prepared the spices, they walked toward the tomb "just after sunrise," wondering who would roll the stone away from the tomb's entrance for them (Mark 16:2–3). Before long, while approaching the tomb, they saw the stone was already gone (Mark 16:4). Their decision to act promptly that morning brought them to the tomb that was wide open because of the miraculous and wonderful resurrection of our Lord Jesus Christ (Mark 16:6).

They were the first to learn that Jesus rose from the dead (Mark 16:6).

Being at the Right Place and Time

By acting promptly to do the right thing, the three women landed at the right place, at the right time! They carried to the disciples and others the good news of the single most significant event in human history. The Apostle Paul put this in perspective: *"If Christ has not been raised, your faith is futile"* (1 Corinthians 15:17).

Further, one of the three women, Mary Magdalene, received the very special honor of being the first person to meet and converse with the resurrected Lord Jesus Christ (Mark 16:9), an honor that escaped the disciples. She ran to the disciples and exclaimed, *"I have seen the Lord!"* (John 20:18).

Wanting to do the right thing, she came prepared to anoint the lifeless body of Jesus with spices. Instead, she had a surprising meeting with the resurrected Jesus Christ in His glorious body—"Mary, no need for your spices, please!"

Leaders are called to do the right thing day after day; sometimes when they do so, a pleasant surprise may be waiting for them!

Discuss from a Christian Leader's Perspective:

1. Do you recall an instance when you did the right thing, and the result was memorable?

2. What hinders us from doing the right thing?

3. Do you recall an instance when you should have done the right thing but failed to do so?

Leaders Act Promptly

Jesus Needed an Honorable Burial

Joseph of Arimathea acted promptly at a very critical time, and there is much we can learn from his example.

> *Joseph of Arimathea, a prominent member of the Council, who was himself waiting for the kingdom of God, went boldly to Pilate and asked for Jesus' body. Pilate was surprised to hear that he was already dead. Summoning the centurion, he asked him if Jesus had already died. When he learned from the centurion that it was so, he gave the body to Joseph. So Joseph bought some linen cloth, took down the body, wrapped it in the linen, and placed it in a tomb cut out of rock. Then he rolled a stone against the entrance of the tomb. (Mark 15:43–46)*

It is clear that Joseph of Arimathea wanted an honorable burial for the body of Jesus after it was taken down from the cross. Prior to this episode, his loyalty and devotion to Jesus were not public (John 19:38). Reports say that he was a wealthy businessman/trader influential enough to be a member of the powerful Sanhedrin, the ruling Council.

He Used His Authority and Influence

Being a prominent member of the ruling Council, he was in a position of influence and authority to do something to ensure an honorable burial for Jesus' lifeless body. He knew it.

If he failed to act, the body of Jesus might have received a dishonorable and distasteful treatment. He had to act fast without hesitation.

Joseph acted so fast that the Roman ruler, Pontius Pilate, who ordered the crucifixion, could not believe Jesus was dead already; Pilate sought verification of Jesus' death through his centurion before granting Joseph's request to carefully take down the body of Jesus for entombment or burial (Mark 15:44).

Perhaps no one else among those who were devoted to Jesus had the access and influence to meet Pilate, the ruler, and accomplish what Joseph did with such promptness. Joseph was aware of what he could do with his influence.

Joseph shed his cloak of secrecy (John 19:38) about his loyalty and devotion to Jesus, and he identified publicly with Him. This was in defiance of the ruling Council that brought about the cruel death of Jesus upon the cross through the Roman ruler, Pontius Pilate. Unknown to us, Joseph might have faced ridicule and paid a price for identifying publicly with Jesus. Joseph must have weighed the consequences and moved ahead, regardless.

Act When Your Influence Is Needed

In this context, Joseph's prompt act of leadership is also a public display of courage on behalf of all who prayed that day for an honorable burial for Jesus. At times like this, leadership calls for extraordinary courage.

Joseph knew what to do. He did what he needed to do. He did not hesitate. He led when it counted, while risking his reputation and facing any possible consequences.

Because of his prompt and decisive act of leadership, he succeeded in giving a very honorable burial/entombment for the body of Jesus. Those who love the Lord Jesus say, thank you!

We need leaders like Joseph who do not hesitate to act courageously and promptly when no one else can. He made a difference when he did, and so can you.

Discuss from a Christian Leader's Perspective:

1. Have you had the chance to use your influence with the public authorities at a critical time for someone's ministry?

2. What might have happened if Joseph did not step up to publicly identify with Jesus and His family?

3. If you are a person of authority in the secular world, are you prepared to be of assistance to Christian ministries that needs legitimate help from authorities?

Pursue Excellence

A culture of excellence in life may enable a Christian leader to take on challenges that he/she otherwise cannot.

Young David Overcomes a National Crisis

The nation of Israel faced an existential threat from the Philistine army when the giant, Goliath, issued a challenge to King Saul and his army (1 Samuel 17:1–11). Youthful David, offended by Goliath's challenge to the nation of Israel (1 Samuel 17:26), and in the absence of a single armed Israeli soldier willing to accept Goliath's challenge for a duel, volunteered to fight him single-handedly using a skill he had perfected earlier in life.

Upon hearing David's offer to fight Goliath, King Saul initially questioned the youth's qualification and ability to fight Goliath, the well-armed, giant Philistine soldier. But, upon hearing young David's spirited assurance,

Saul said to David, "Go, and the LORD be with you."

Then Saul dressed David in his own tunic. He put a coat of armor on him and a bronze helmet on his head. David fastened on his sword over the tunic and tried walking around, because he was not used to them.

"I cannot go in these," he said to Saul, "because I am not used to them." So he took them off. Then he took his staff in his hand, chose five smooth stones from the stream, put them in the pouch of his shepherd's bag and, with his sling in his hand, approached the Philistine. (1 Samuel 17:37–40)

As the Philistine [Goliath] moved closer to attack him, David ran quickly toward the battle line to meet him. Reaching into his bag and taking out a stone, he slung it and struck the Philistine on the forehead. The stone sank into his forehead, and he fell face down on the ground. (1 Samuel 17:48–49)

A Shepherd Boy Perfects a Dependable Skill

David chose a sling as his weapon of choice against a man who caused the men of the Israeli army to flee at his very sight (1 Samuel 17:24). David's faith in God, and his confidence in his skill in the use of the sling, outweighed the threat and intimidation posed by the giant and his weaponry.

During his days as a shepherd boy grazing sheep in grassy fields, David must have developed excellence in the use of the sling, almost to perfection. He might have needed the skill to protect his sheep, or it might have been just a boyish hobby.

It should be noted that young David turned down the king's bulky personal armor and weapons after he tried them on. For David, they paled in comparison to his dependable and excellent skill with the sling.

A lesson from young David: Leaders ought to devote time and effort to perfect their God-given skills. You never know when you will be called upon as a leader to use the skills you have perfected over time. David volunteered to employ his excellent skill at the time of a grave national crisis and emerged with legendary success.

Apostle Paul Was a Skilled Pharisee

In earlier days, when the Apostle Paul was diligently preparing to become a Pharisee, skilled in the Jewish scriptures and Mosaic Law, he did not anticipate that one day God would use his excellent knowledge of the Mosaic Law and reasoning skills as an apostle of Jesus Christ.

The Apostle Paul's knowledge of the law and logical skills of argument were uniquely handy while debating both Jews and non-Jews, and while writing to Roman, Corinthian, and other first-century church congregations. His epistles to those first-century churches have convinced seekers and skeptics and have strengthened the worldwide Church and its leaders for more than 2,000 years.

Faith, the Holy Spirit, and the Grace of God

In the Bible, the faith of David and Paul stand out. They were led by the Holy Spirit, and they served as leaders with an abundance of God's grace. God called on their excellent skills when mediocrity wouldn't cut it.

As leaders, pursue excellence; you never know when and how God will use your excellent skills in His service.

Discuss from a Christian Leader's Perspective:

1. Like David, do you excel in something, or are you preparing to excel in something to be of value to the Kingdom?

2. How does Paul motivate you to excel in something? How do you respond?

3. What may be your excellent skills that you are able to devote to the ministry?

How Moses Dealt with Rebellion

"They Are Almost Ready to Stone Me"

"They are almost ready to stone me" (Exodus 17:4) is a perfect description of a rebellion against a leader. These were the alarming words of Moses while approaching God for help, when the people of Israel turned rebellious. Although Moses' words sound ominous, they were NOT a prelude to "Lord, I quit. I am out of here." Here is what happened:

> *The whole Israelite community set out from the Desert of Sin … camped at Rephidim, but there was no water for the people to drink. So they quarreled with Moses and said, "Give us water to drink."*
>
> *Moses replied, "Why do you quarrel with me? Why do you put the LORD to the test?"*
>
> *But the people were thirsty for water there, and they grumbled against Moses. They said, "Why did you bring us up out of Egypt to make us and our children and livestock die of thirst?"*
>
> *Then Moses cried out to the LORD, "What am I to do with these people? They are almost ready to stone me."* (Exodus 17:1–4)

Moses was not the last leader to face a rebellion. In most cases, a leader's words or deeds may have contributed to the rebellion. But we know that Moses was not the cause of the lack of water. As their leader, Moses could see their plight and sympathize with his people, but he was totally helpless in getting them water without God's help in the dry and desolate land around them.

Were the people rebelling against Moses? Since God was the provider for the people of Israel when Moses led them out of Egypt, this was a rebellion against God; Moses understood that.

Moses' Response to the Rebellion

Moses' complaint to God, "They are almost ready to stone me," is a call for help. It has a "God-I-desperately-need-your-help-now" tone to it.

Moses had seen God come through again and again for His people. He saw God come down hard with plagues upon Egypt, when Pharaoh would not let His people go. He saw God progressively pressure Pharaoh until he ultimately let the people of Israel leave Egypt. Later, Moses saw God's people cross the Red Sea miraculously, and he witnessed Pharaoh's army go under the waters of the Red Sea while it was pursuing God's people.

With a fresh memory of these recent actions of God on behalf of His people, Moses approached God, knowing He would deliver. He also knew God cared for His people and would come through. Thus, his response to the rebellion was to approach God for help instead of giving up on the people and walking away—in other words, quitting was not an option.

Moses Neither Quit nor Tried to Quit

Although Moses accepted the task reluctantly at the burning bush (Exodus chapters 3 and 4), he showed total commitment to his task of leading God's people out of Egypt to the Promised Land. For example, in Egypt, Moses was locked in a struggle with the mighty Pharaoh to free God's people. The intensity of Moses' struggle with Pharaoh became evident when Pharaoh was angry at Moses after the ninth plague, and he declared that he would kill Moses if he saw him ever again (Exodus 10:28–29). Moses could have chosen to quit upon hearing the death threat from the mighty ruthless ruler, but he did not.

For many leaders in Moses' place, the rebellion could have easily triggered anger and disappointment with God or with the nation of Israel or both, and it may have instigated them to quit. However, when Moses approached God, he did not say, "I quit"; instead, he said, "What should I do with these people?" (verse 4 in the passage above). These words of Moses imply that he was looking for a solution from God and declared his willingness to continue to lead the people and do God's bidding.

Knowing God Made the Difference for Moses

Moses' deep knowledge of God prevented him from becoming angry and discouraged by the rebellion, because he understood that the people rebelled against God. Further, knowing God, Moses knew he could get help from Him. After Moses' request for help, God intervened miraculously to provide water for the whole nation of Israel in the dry and desolate place (Exodus 17:5–6). God came through once more.

After this incident, Moses continued to serve as a remarkable leader for a total of forty years from the time God assigned him the task. He successfully brought the nation of Israel to the edge of the Promised Land as he was tasked to do by God; no wonder he is commended and honored across the Bible for his faithfulness, his humility, and his accomplishments.

So how did Moses handle the rebellion? First, he correctly recognized it to be a rebellion against God and not against himself. Second, he chose not to quit leading God's people or to walk away because of the rebellion. Third, knowing God as well as he did, he turned to God, who alone could help him and his people under the circumstances to get them water.

Finally, without being sidetracked by the rebellion, under God's guidance, Moses continued as their leader until the almost impossible task that God assigned to him was complete. When Moses successfully completed his task near the end of his earthly life, we know that God was immensely pleased with him.

Discuss from a Christian Leader's Perspective:

1. Have you faced rebellion? How did you deal with it?

2. In a position of leadership, if you faced rebellion, how would you deal with it, given what Moses did?

3. Why do people rebel in a Christian organization?

LESSON 11

The Team of Moses and Aaron Survived

When Moses and his older brother Aaron were both in their eighties, God assigned them to a team with a very demanding, long-lasting, almost impossible task. Working together for 40 years, they successfully completed their assigned task of bringing Israel to the River Jordan, across from the Promised Land, when the nation was ready to enter it.

We know for certain that Moses' work pleased God, who called him *"more humble than anyone else on the face of the earth"* (Numbers 12:3) and *"faithful in all my house"* (v. 7). After his death, the Bible also records: *"Since then, no prophet has risen in Israel like Moses, whom the LORD knew face to face"* (Deuteronomy 34:10).

Moses' Personality Style Matched His Leadership Task

At the "bush," Moses was not eager to accept God's call to lead Israel out of Egypt to the Promised Land (Exodus 3:7–10). Instead, Moses pleaded, "Please send someone else" (Exodus 4:13). God ignored his plea and sent Moses on his way to Egypt to lead Israel, estimated at about two million people, to the Promised Land. God assigned Moses' brother Aaron as his assistant and spokesman, thereby creating a team of two brothers (Exodus 4:15–16).

DISC Explains Moses' Leadership Style

If you are familiar with either the Classic or Biblical DISC personality profiles/styles, you may recognize that Moses displayed qual-

53

ities of both "D" and "C" personality styles (see the Appendix at the end of this chapter for more information on DISC personality types).

As a "D" personality, he was decisive, determined, goal directed, not easily pushed around by others, and comfortable and at peace with his position of authority and leadership for about 40 years.

As a "C," he was capable of processing volumes of data (Exodus 18:17–23), analytical in thinking, logical, and capable of reasoning with the best; his reasoned plea to God to spare the life of Israel on Mount Sinai, when God caught them worshiping an idol, is a fine example of his calm reasoning skills under pressure (Exodus 32:11–14).

Moses' task of leading a nation of about two million unruly people (God described them as "stiff-necked people," Exodus 32:9) through the Sinai desert, with no permanent land to call their own, must have been extremely challenging—perhaps the most difficult leadership task in recorded history. It called for prolonged dedication and conscientiousness on the part of Moses; these are qualities found in a combination of "D" and "C" personality styles.

Aaron Failed Once but Thrived as High Priest

At Mount Sinai, when Moses was on the top of the mountain conversing with God, Aaron was the de facto leader for 40 days. Aaron failed precipitously at this temporary leadership task by enabling the worship of a golden calf demanded by the people he was expected to "lead." When Moses came down the mountain to see what was going on, *"Moses saw that the people were running wild and that **Aaron had let them get out of control** and so become a laughingstock to their enemies"* (Exodus 32:25).

At the first meeting between the brothers after the disastrous failure of Aaron, Moses asked his older brother, *"**What did these peo-***

ple do to you, that you led them into such great sin?" (Exodus 33:21). The wording of this question is a clue to Aaron's personality style.

The question implies that a) Aaron could be pushed by others to do things that are wrong and sinful, b) he could be influenced by others, and c) he could succumb to pressures from others. Thus, the wording of the question by Moses reveals that Aaron lacked key features of the "D" personality style.

On the DISC personality style framework, Aaron appears to be exhibit "I" personality style, which is associated with good communication skills and people orientation. God confirmed the communication skills of Aaron when God said this to Moses: *"What about your brother, Aaron the Levite? I know he can speak well.... He will speak to the people for you, and it will be as if he were your mouth and as if you were God to him"* (Exodus 4:14–16).

They Worked through Personality Differences

At Mount Sinai, Aaron failed as a leader when Moses was gone 40 days. This is what Moses said about that "golden calf" episode of Aaron:

> And the LORD was angry enough with Aaron to destroy him, but at that time I prayed for Aaron too. Also I took that sinful thing of yours, the calf you had made, and burned it in the fire. Then I crushed it and ground it to powder as fine as dust and threw the dust into a stream that flowed down the mountain. (Deuteronomy 9:20–21)

When God asked Moses to anoint Aaron as the first priest to the nation (Exodus 40:13), **Moses did not object** to it by saying, "He led the entire nation away from you by enabling them to worship a golden calf that he crafted. He is unfit, Lord, why not appoint someone else?"

When siblings or spouses are as different as Moses and Aaron, they may lack respect for each other or may even dislike each other. Moses and Aaron should inspire team members, couples, and siblings to work together through mutual respect even when their personalities are far apart. In the case of Moses and Aaron, God put them together knowing they had different personalities and associated skills (Exodus 4:14–16).

Team members with vastly different personality styles may never understand each other fully. To overcome this, make extra attempts to understand members of your team with personality styles that are unlike yours, and make concessions to accommodate a team member endowed with a personality style that is different from yours.

If Moses and Aaron with vastly different personality styles could work together to complete their difficult task successfully over a period of 40 years, anyone can.

Lesson 11 Appendix

In this Appendix, the four personality types of Biblical DISC are defined concisely using information in the website for Lead Like Jesus (Biblical DISC assessment). For more information, go to this website (https://www.leadlikejesus.com/disc) and similar websites on DISC personality types.

Type D: Dominance	Daring, decisive, direct, persistent, problem solver, etc.
Type I: Influencing	Enthusiastic, optimistic, sociable, trusting, etc.
Type S: Steadiness	Friendly, good listener, team player, understanding, etc.
Type C: Conscientious	Accurate, analytical, compliant, fact finder, logical, objective, etc.

Discuss from a Christian Leader's Perspective:

1. What made Moses and Aaron incompatible?

2. Given their different personality styles, how did they succeed in working together for 40 years?

3. Have you experienced incompatibility between teammates that caused problems for team performance? What could you learn from Moses to overcome such problems?

How Moses Avoided Deadly Distractions

Moses Was Denied Entry into the Promised Land

God's decision to deny Moses entry into the Promised Land was significant (Numbers 20:12–13), because God reminded Moses of this decision multiple times (Numbers 20:24; Numbers 27:14; Deuteronomy 32:51–52). Further, it is noted in Psalm 106:32, where it says, *"By the waters of Meribah they* [the nation of Israel] *angered the* LORD, *and trouble came to Moses because of them."*

After God's decision (or God's will) was made known to Moses that he was being denied entry into the Promised Land because of what happened at Meribah, Moses asked God to grant him the privilege of going into the Promised Land on the other side of the River Jordan. This is how Moses described to his people his personal request to God:

> At that time I pleaded with the Lord: "Sovereign Lord, you have begun to show to your servant your greatness and your strong hand. For what god is there in heaven or on earth who can do the deeds and mighty works you do? Let me go over and see the good land beyond the Jordan—that fine hill country and Lebanon."

> But because of you the Lord was angry with me and would not listen to me. "That is enough," the Lord said. "Do not speak to me anymore about this matter. Go up to the top of Pisgah and look west and north and south and east. Look at the land with your own eyes, since you

are not going to cross this Jordan. But commission Joshua, and encourage and strengthen him, for he will lead this people across and will cause them to inherit the land that you will see." (Deuteronomy 3:23–28)

This is the record of Moses' appeal to God for a chance to go into the Promised Land. Moses, upon knowing God's decision to keep him out, could have reacted or responded negatively, just as many of us do.

However, it is evident from the recorded history in Exodus through Deuteronomy that Moses accepted God's will as a matter of fact. With unwavering positive intent, he devoted himself totally to the difficult task of leading the nation of Israel to the edge of the Promised Land. He did not allow God's decision to distract him from his main calling.

Moses Avoids Eight Deadly Distractions

The evidence in the Bible points to Moses gracefully accepting God's decision (or call it God's will). Therefore, we do not see the following eight distractions in Moses' life:

1. There is no record of Moses being disheartened or discouraged by God's decision.

2. There is no record of Moses being saddened by it.

3. There is no record of Moses worrying about it.

4. There is no record of Moses claiming he was denied what he deserved.

5. There is no record of Moses claiming he earned the right to enter the Promised Land.

6. There is no record of Moses considering God's decision as unfair.

7. There is no record of Moses complaining about God to others.

8. There is no record of Moses paying attention to people's opinion on this matter.

Moses Accepted God's Will as a Matter of Fact

A leader focused on his/her main cause or calling must learn to recognize similar potential distractions in his/her life and bury them as soon as possible. If not, the above list of uncontrolled distractions can disable and diminish a leader. Consequently, a leader may fail to accomplish his/her ultimate calling.

Even if you are not a leader, these eight distractions can also diminish and disable your ability to live a God-intended fulfilled life.

As a Christian leader focused on your calling, do you promptly attempt to bury these **Eight Deadly Distractions** when they pop up in your life?

Discuss from a Christian Leader's Perspective:

1. Do you think that after everything Moses did, he deserved to enter the Promised Land, at least for a short time?

2. Was God "fair" to Moses? Was Moses entitled to enter the Promised Land?

3. How do you deal with major disappointments in life and ministry? What would you do differently now after knowing how Moses handled God's decision?

LESSON 13

The Grateful Leader

Give Thanks Always

In the first chapter of Romans, the Apostle Paul addresses the sinfulness of people who failed to glorify God and failed to thank Him:

> For although they knew God, they neither glorified him as God **nor gave thanks to him**, but their thinking became futile and their foolish hearts were darkened. (Romans 1:21).

> They have become filled with every kind of wickedness, evil, greed and depravity. They are full of envy, murder, strife, deceit and malice. (Romans 1:29)

Giving thanks to God is a vital part of our relationship with Him, and it may reveal our closeness to Him. It is not surprising that the Apostle Paul, through his many epistles to churches, encourages all of us to give thanks to God in all circumstances. Here are three examples of his instruction on thanksgiving from his epistles to three different churches:

> Give thanks in all circumstances; for this is God's will for you in Christ Jesus. (1 Thessalonians 5:18)

> Always giving thanks to God the Father for everything, in the name of our Lord Jesus Christ. (Ephesians 5:20)

> Let the message of Christ dwell among you richly as you teach and admonish one another with all wisdom through psalms, hymns, and songs from the Spirit, singing to God with gratitude in your hearts. (Colossians 3:16)

These words of the Apostle Paul may make us wonder if we are thanking God as we ought to. Are we busy pushing "I want" lists to God in our prayers, however legitimate they may be, without thanking Him? What made it easy for Paul to be profusely thankful to God? He was aware God loved him. He knew God was a caring father to him under all circumstances. He said:

> For I am convinced that neither death nor life, neither angels nor demons, neither the present nor the future, nor any powers, neither height nor depth, nor anything else in all creation, will be able to separate us from the love of God that is in Christ Jesus our Lord. (Romans 8:38–39)

Thanking God in "All Circumstances"

All the circumstances in our lives fall between two extremes: the desirable and the undesirable. We pray for and welcome those circumstances that are closer to the desirable extreme in our lives but shun circumstances that are closer to the other extreme.

Paul says to thank God regardless of the desirability of your circumstances. Is it possible to do so? Paul is being truthful when he asks us to be thankful in "all circumstances." He was in prison while writing some of his famous letters including the "Epistle of Joy," as the epistle of Philippians is described by some. This epistle is peppered with the terms "joy" and "rejoice," even though it was written during his unjust imprisonment.

Apostle Paul does not complain that his time in the prison was a disaster for his vigorous church-planting ministry; instead, he says even his prison guards in Rome were aware of "his imprisonment for Christ":

> I want you to know, brothers, that what has happened to me [being in prison] has really served to advance the gospel, so that it has become known throughout the whole imperial

guard and to all the rest that my imprisonment is for Christ. (Philippians 1:12–13)

Paul was a leader and an itinerant missionary who planted churches in various cities along his mission trips. Constrained to a life in prison, first in Caesarea and later in Rome, he could not be the itinerant church planter he longed to be. Yet, in his epistles, he was thankful to God without complaining, while encouraging readers to be thankful; through those epistles he has been preaching and teaching about Jesus Christ for more than 2,000 years.

Daniel Thanked God under Threat of Execution

The Apostle Paul is not alone in grasping the vital role of thanksgiving in his relationship with God. The Bible records that during Daniel's Babylonian exile from Jerusalem, with the knowledge of King Darius' decree prohibiting prayers to any god, Daniel prayed and thanked God in view of others:

*Now when Daniel learned that the decree had been published, he went home to his upstairs room where the windows opened toward Jerusalem. Three times a day he got down on his knees and prayed, **giving thanks to his God,** just as he had done before.* (Daniel 6:10)

The king's prohibition against prayers to God was accompanied by a deadly consequence; violators were thrown into the lions' den (Daniel 6:10–13).

Well-known leaders such as the Apostle Paul and Daniel were generously thankful to God in all circumstances; are you? You can never thank God too much! Try it!

Leaders such as Paul and Daniel understood the special and critical need to thank God to continue to serve Him as leaders.

Discuss from a Christian Leader's Perspective:

1. Were Paul and Daniel unrealistic in their dealings with God?

2. What prevents you from giving thanks to God in all circumstances as practiced by Paul and Daniel?

3. Can you think of a circumstance in which you were thankful but could have justified being angry and upset with God? Or the reverse?

God Gave Aaron a Second Chance

Aaron Fell

Aaron was approached by people who asked him to *"Come make us gods who shall go before us"* (Exodus 32:1) while their leader, Moses, was gone for a meeting with God on Mt. Sinai for 40 long days. Aaron did not resist; instead, he almost immediately obliged them with a well-publicized effort to make a golden calf for the nation to worship:

> *Aaron answered them, "Take off the gold earrings that your wives, your sons and your daughters are wearing, and bring them to me." So all the people took off their earrings and brought them to Aaron. He took what they handed him and made it into an idol cast in the shape of a calf, fashioning it with a tool. Then they said, "These are your gods, Israel, who brought you up out of Egypt."*

> *When Aaron saw this, he built an altar in front of the calf and announced, "Tomorrow there will be a festival to the* LORD.*" So the next day the people rose early and sacrificed burnt offerings and presented fellowship offerings. Afterward they sat down to eat and drink and got up to indulge in revelry.* (Exodus 32:2–6)

The Consequence of Aaron's Fall

While Moses was still conversing with God on the top of Mt. Sinai, God noticed Aaron's golden calf at the bottom of the mountain and its worship by God's people, whom He brought out of Egypt: *"I have seen these people,"* the LORD *said to Moses, "and they are a stiff-necked people. Now leave me alone so that my anger may burn against them and that I may destroy them. Then I will make you into a great nation"* (Exodus 32:9–10).

God was ready to destroy the calf-worshipping nation of Israel—the descendants of Abraham—on their way to the Promised Land. When God said, "I will make a great nation of you," He offered to replace the nation of Israel with future descendants of Moses.

Promptly, Moses ducked God's offer to make his descendants a great nation at the expense of Abraham's descendants. Instead, unselfishly, he pleaded with God for mercy and forgiveness for the calf-worshiping descendants of Abraham, whom he had been leading to the Promised Land. He succeeded in convincing God with his unselfish pleas on behalf of the people he was called to lead.

What Moses Thought of Aaron's Fall

Moses was obviously distressed by his brother Aaron's lapse that almost got the nation of Israel destroyed. Therefore, Moses asked Aaron after the debacle, *"What did these people do to you, that **you led them into such great sin?**"* (Exodus 32:21).

Moses' question implies that he was aware that Aaron could be easily swayed or pushed around by others to commit a gravely sinful act. He could also be made to compromise the very things that should never be compromised. Additionally, Moses' question implies that his brother succumbed to pressure, or he was attempting to please others, or he was unfit to lead, or a combination of these weaknesses.

God Gives Aaron a Significant Second Chance

Surprisingly, not very long after Aaron fell and Moses intervened to save the nation from destruction, God said this to Moses:

"Bring Aaron and his sons to the entrance to the tent of meeting and wash them with water. Then dress Aaron in the sacred garments, anoint him and consecrate him so he may serve me as priest." ... Moses did everything just as the LORD commanded him. (Exodus 40:12–13, 16)

This direction to Moses to anoint Aaron as the nation's foremost priest is evidence that Aaron had repented, God had forgiven him, and he was granted a significant second chance.

It would NOT surprise anyone if Moses thought Aaron was unfit to be the nation's premier priest after he enabled the nation to worship a golden calf that brought the wrath of God upon the nation and that some died as a consequence (Exodus 32:35).

Moses Accepts Aaron's Priesthood after the Fall

Given Aaron's fall and its consequence, it is notable that Moses did not express to God any objection to anointing Aaron as the nation's priest; instead, he promptly fulfilled God's directions to anoint Aaron as the nation's first and foremost priest (Exodus 40:16). Therefore, we can infer this: Moses, with a personal knowledge of Aaron's repentance, forgave Aaron, and when God instructed him, he was ready to give Aaron a second chance as the nation's premier priest.

Aaron made good use of his second chance, and as we read in Exodus and Numbers, he never squandered it before his death (Numbers 20:25-29)—a well-deserved second chance.

Wow!

God gave Aaron a second chance, and Moses did, too. As a leader, would you give a second chance to a repentant colleague/partner/staff member?

Discuss from a Christian Leader's Perspective:

1. Can you think of someone in your life who deserves a second chance from you or from people you know, but did not get one?

2. How does the God-given second chance to Aaron help your understanding of how God works?

3. What makes it hard for you to give second chances to others?

The Proactive Path of Leaders

There is a proactive path that will glorify God. We see a vivid example in scripture:

> *Some men came carrying a paralyzed man on a mat and tried to take him into the house to lay him before Jesus. When they could not find a way to do this because of the crowd, they went up on the roof and lowered him on his mat through the tiles into the middle of the crowd, right in front of Jesus.*
>
> *When Jesus saw their faith, he said, "Friend, your sins are forgiven."* (Luke 5:18–20)
>
> *So he [Jesus] said to the paralyzed man, "I tell you, get up, take your mat and go home." Immediately he stood up in front of them, took what he had been lying on and went home praising God. Everyone was amazed and gave praise to God. They were filled with awe and said, "We have seen remarkable things today."* (Luke 5:24–26)

A team of men made an extraordinary effort, and when they reached their goal, against extraordinary obstacles, a paralyzed man was healed by Jesus. Many witnesses to the healing "glorified God and were filled with awe."

When the men started on their extraordinary journey to bring their friend to Jesus, they most likely did not consider the many people who would glorify God upon witnessing the healing of their friend by Jesus.

The men vividly showed us: "Make extraordinary efforts to bring people to Jesus Christ for healing or salvation, and witness God being glorified."

A Non-traditional and Proactive Solution

When the men could not get access to Jesus Christ seated inside the house, they had at least three **traditional options**:

1. To wait until the crowd began to leave the house and then enter the house.

2. To wait for Jesus to walk out of the house eventually, and then seek healing for their friend.

3. To blame the crowd, and without waiting, abandon their goal to take the sick man to Jesus Christ for healing. That is, retreat or quit.

Traditional options 1 and 2 would have needed patience, while option 3 would have shown lack of resolve and passivity. The men chose not to use any of the traditional options, but instead, they went for a non-traditional and risky option to reach Jesus Christ right away, and they succeeded.

Successfully taking the sick man to Jesus Christ by lowering him through the roof was creative and original; perhaps no one in history ever thought of doing so before them. It also qualifies as an extraordinarily proactive option.

There are always obstacles on the path to any predetermined goal. How we address the obstacles on the path to our goal separates the proactive team/leader from those who are not.

Undertaking a Manageable Risk

When overcoming obstacles, extraordinary options may involve a higher degree of risk. Yes, this team took on added risk while climbing up to the roof, removing it, and lowering the sick friend down into the house. The risk assumed by the group involved potential injury to the team itself, to the sick friend, to Jesus Christ below, and to the people around Him—the people inside the house could have suffered injury from falling debris or falling men.

The team succeeded in not injuring anyone. The risky and proactive episode turned out all right; it was a manageable risk.

Overcoming Extraordinary Obstacles

The Bible does not identify a leader of the team that accomplished its goal using an extraordinary solution. Most likely, the men had a leader who took them through an extraordinary and proactive path to channel the team's energy to successfully attain their goal.

As a leader, are you prepared to take proactive, non-traditional solutions while pursuing your team's or your organization's goal if faced with an obstacle that would defy ordinary solutions?

Discuss from a Christian Leader's Perspective:

1. Have you or someone known to you ever displayed the kind of leadership that accomplished the goal of taking a sick man to Jesus Christ against almost impossible odds?

2. How would you motivate a team to attempt something like the above?

3. Jesus did not make the team's task any easier. Is there a message for proactive leaders today?

Lessons from Jesus on Leadership

Lesson

What Jesus Expects from Leaders

Jesus Issues a Strong Warning

Jesus, during his ministry, was often confronted by the teachers of the law and Pharisees. He warned them often; here is one of the warnings addressed to them in Matthew 23:23–24:

> "Woe to you, teachers of the law and Pharisees, you hypocrites! You give a tenth of your spices—mint, dill and cumin. But you have neglected the more important matters of the law—justice, mercy and faithfulness. You should have practiced the latter, without neglecting the former. You blind guides! You strain out a gnat but swallow a camel."

Jesus warned the Pharisees and other leaders concerning the pursuit of trivial rules in the mistaken hope of EARNING their RIGHT to enter the Kingdom of God. He mentioned the futility of striving to keep these trivial rules at the expense of three important spiritual qualities that were neglected or compromised by those leaders. These three spiritual qualities of leaders transcend time; they are just as important today as they were when Jesus uttered them.

So what did Jesus say leaders must do? He said leaders must pursue justice, mercy, and faithfulness. What do these spiritual qualities mean, and how do they apply to Christian leaders today?

Jesus Expects Justice

What is justice? It is the morally and ethically fair treatment of others when one is in a position of authority to make decisions that affect others.

How is justice evident in a leader's life? Proverbs 29:7 says, *"The righteous care about justice for the poor, but the wicked have no such concern."*

Routinely, justice or injustice for the poor is administered by the decisions of leaders in positions of authority.

Leaders must be conscious of the fact that it is quite easy for leaders and the powerful to neglect justice in their actions affecting the poor and the defenseless. Remember, according to the verse above, the Pharisees were able to ignore justice, and they got away with it—Jesus appeared to be the only one confronting them.

The verse also includes the ominous statement that a leader who is unjust toward the poor is "wicked"; it is not a label that a true Christian leader would want.

Jesus Expects Mercy

How is mercy evident in a leader's life? Proverbs 18:23 says, *"The poor plead for mercy, but the rich answer harshly."*

The term "rich" could include leaders and people in positions of authority who are often wealthy. Just as we noted above, mercy is also defined in the context of how rich and powerful leaders treat the poor and the defenseless. In life, the poor are often placed in situations where they are at the mercy of the decisions or actions of leaders and/or people in authority.

By their conduct toward the poor and the defenseless, leaders can demonstrate mercy or the lack of it. The verse also notes that leaders and others in authority, when they lack mercy, could be "harsh" in the treatment of the poor and the defenseless. Merciful treatment takes away the harshness.

As Christian leaders, seek God's grace to display mercy in your relationships with poor, weak, and defenseless people in your life and/or those you encounter.

Jesus Expects Faithfulness

How is faithfulness evident in a leader's life? Speaking of God, the author of Psalm 91:4 says, *"His faithfulness will be your shield and rampart."*

"Rampart" refers to the protective wall surrounding an ancient town to keep out brutal invaders. A shield is a personal protective tool.

Faithful leaders protect those they lead as an expression of their faithfulness. Faithful leaders would not abandon their followers when they need the protection of leaders. Moses protected the nation of Israel from God's wrath when he was in conversation with God on Mount Sinai (Exodus 32:9–14). Leaders have an obligation to protect those they lead.

Jesus called Pharisees and other leaders "blind guides," meaning they can go astray while taking their followers with them; this is not the mark of a faithful leader. The term "blind guides" also implies they cannot see or teach what is true; consequently, unlike faithful leaders, they can mislead or misdirect their followers.

In admonishing the Pharisees, Jesus revealed that He expects justice, mercy, and faithfulness from Christian leaders.

Discuss from a Christian Leader's Perspective:

1. Can you think of instances in which Christian leaders make decisions that compromise justice, mercy, and faithfulness?

2. Have you seen the compromise of justice, mercy, and faithfulness by Christian leaders? What do you think caused them to compromise what Jesus expects from leaders?

3. What could Christian organizations do to ensure their leaders are less likely to compromise justice, mercy, and faithfulness?

Jesus Condemns Hypocritical Leaders

Don't Do What the Hypocrites Do

Chapter 23 of Matthew's Gospel records Jesus' outrage and strong condemnation of the hypocrisy of leaders. It also gives us a glimpse of the consequences of leaders' hypocrisy for those who follow them.

Referring to the conduct of the Pharisees and teachers of the law, early in the chapter, Jesus summarized His condemnation of their hypocrisy by saying to His listeners and disciples, *"Do not do what they do, for they do not practice what they preach"* (Matthew 23:3).

By the way, "they do not practice what they preach" is a textbook definition for hypocrisy.

This problem of leaders teaching one thing and living another is a timeless problem; we can see this around us today. The temptation facing leaders to say one thing and do another is always present.

It is easy for leaders to teach, but it is much harder for leaders to practice what they teach. It was true when Jesus condemned it, and it is true among leaders today.

Do You Practice What You Teach?

Referring to hypocritical leaders/teachers, when Jesus said, "Do not do what they do," His words beg the question, "How does the listener know what the leaders/teachers do?" Clearly, by implication, Jesus is telling His listeners that they need to pay attention to what their leaders/teachers do. Thus, Jesus is placing a burden on those being taught—they are to watch their teachers to see if they practice what they teach.

Jesus was instructing His listeners that the lives and actions of hypocritical leaders should not guide them when their behaviors are INCONSISTENT with their own teachings.

The Consequences of Leaders' Hypocrisy

> *"Woe to you, teachers of the law and Pharisees, you hypocrites! You shut the door of the kingdom of heaven in people's faces. You yourselves do not enter, nor will you let those enter who are trying to."* (Matthew 23:13)

In the above passage, a warning was directed to the hypocritical Pharisees and other leaders/teachers who assumed that they had EARNED their right to enter the kingdom of heaven. But Jesus told them otherwise.

Further, Jesus warned that hypocritical leaders and teachers could lead their followers away from the Kingdom of Heaven ("You shut the door of the kingdom in people's faces ... nor will you let those enter who are trying to" (vs. 13)). In other words, Jesus implied, "Watch out for hypocritical teachers."

From this encounter of Jesus with Pharisees and teachers of the law, we learn, in no uncertain terms, that Jesus wants leaders to be authentic and transparent, without a trace of hypocrisy. If not, leaders and their followers may NOT enter the kingdom of heaven that Jesus has prepared for His followers (Matthew 4:17).

Jesus asks Christian leaders and teachers: "Do you practice what you preach?"

Discuss from a Christian Leader's Perspective:

1. As a leader, what are the most difficult subjects to practice but easy to preach or teach?

2. Why are you failing to practice what you teach?

3. Can you think of a leader who practiced what he taught under very difficult circumstances? (On the other hand, it should not be hard to find a leader who does not practice what he preaches.)

Jesus Saw Greed and Hypocrisy in Leaders

"Woe to you, teachers of the law and Pharisees, you hypocrites! You clean the outside of the cup and dish, but inside they are full of greed and self-indulgence. (Matthew 23:25)

The Magnified Sins of Leaders

Jesus told the Pharisees to clean up their act. He said, *"Blind Pharisee! First clean the inside of the cup and dish, and then the outside also will be clean"* (Matthew 23:26).

This is a harsh but true message from Jesus to leaders. Jesus told the Pharisees they could not hide their greed and self-indulgence with their polished exterior. Instead, they needed victory over both these sins.

While Jesus and others could see a leader's greed and self-indulgence, the danger is that it may not be obvious to the leader.

Greed and self-indulgence are garden-variety sins of all sinners; we need divine help to see greed and self-indulgence in our thoughts and actions. Further, we need divine help to have victory over them both every day.

Leaders and people in authority have added temptations and opportunities to magnify their greed and self-indulgence because of their position; they have a greater need for divine help.

Greed in Leaders

Jesus was not the first to note greed among leaders in the Bible. Jeremiah warns that greed is a pervasive problem that afflicted even prophets and priests: *"From the least to the greatest, all are **greedy** for gain; prophets and priests alike, all practice deceit"* (Jeremiah 6:13).

Remember, prophets and priests were leaders in their days. Ezekiel also saw the hypocrisy that Jesus admonishes.

> *"My people come to you [LORD], as they usually do, and sit before you to hear your words, but they do not put them into practice. Their mouths speak of love, but their hearts are greedy for unjust gain."* (Ezekiel 33:31)

Ezekiel saw greed hiding behind hypocritical words of people around him. Note that Ezekiel's **"unjust gain"** is a good definition of greed.

No individual acknowledges his/her own greed because of the bad reputation it has. Therefore, greed tends to hide behind a hypocritical exterior just as Jesus warned. Thus, greed and hypocrisy go together.

The Fuel for Self-Indulgence

Greed is not an end in itself. It serves as the fuel for luxury and self-indulgence. Speaking of rich oppressors admonished in the epistle of James, the author says: *"You have lived on earth in luxury and self-indulgence"* (James 5:5). Self-indulgence is the gratification of excessive unrestrained desires.

Self-indulgence expresses itself in many ways. Jesus noted one aspect of the self-indulgent conduct of Pharisees when He said,

> *"Everything they do is done for people to see: They make their phylacteries wide and the tassels on their garments long; they love the place of honor at banquets and the most*

important seats in the synagogues; they love to be greeted with respect in the marketplaces and to be called 'Rabbi' by others." (Matthew 23:5–7)

We cannot absolve ourselves of these very same self-indulgent tendencies. We need constant divine help to overcome similar tendencies. Remember, leaders have a magnified temptation and opportunity to be self-indulgent than the average believer.

The good news is that Jesus, who saw greed and self-indulgence hiding behind the polished exteriors of Pharisees, offers us victory over both.

As a leader, what would Jesus say about your personal victory over greed and self-indulgence? Where do you need His help?

Discuss from a Christian Leader's Perspective:

1. What forms of greed and self-indulgence do you detect in yourself and other leaders?

2. Do you think Jesus identified the two major reasons why Christian leaders fall today?

3. Jesus addressed the greed and self-indulgence of teachers of the law and Pharisees of his time. Do they apply to Christian leaders today? Why or why not?

A Biblical Perspective on Handling Dissent

Jesus used the "prodigal son" parable to convey to His believers the unique qualities of God the Father. Teachers and preachers have used this parable to communicate to their listeners the unparalleled loving, merciful, and gracious nature of God the Father. In the parable, the father eagerly awaited his "lost" son, enthusiastically forgave his undeserving son, and celebrated his repentance and his voluntary return home.

> *"But while he was still a long way off, his father saw him and was filled with compassion for him; he ran to his son, threw his arms around him and kissed him. The son said to him, 'Father, I have sinned against heaven and against you. I am no longer worthy to be called your son.' But the father said to his servants, 'Quick! Bring the best robe and put it on him. Put a ring on his finger and sandals on his feet. Bring the fattened calf and kill it. Let's have a feast and celebrate.'"*
> (Luke 15:20–23)

Offended by Father's Mercy

The older son in the parable was offended by the merciful and gracious decision of his father to the benefit of his younger brother. What can we learn from the older son's conduct and his father's response to him in the parable? We can learn how the father handled dissent from his faithful son.

> *"Meanwhile, the older son was in the field. When he came near the house, he heard music and dancing. So he called*

one of the servants and asked him what was going on. 'Your brother has come,' he replied, 'and your father has killed the fattened calf because he has him back safe and sound.'" (Luke 15:25–27)

But the older son was angry and refused to go in. His father came out and entreated him. His answer to his father was,

"Look! All these years I've been slaving for you and never disobeyed your orders. Yet you never gave me even a young goat so I could celebrate with my friends. But when this son of yours who has squandered your property with prostitutes comes home, you kill the fattened calf for him!" (Luke 15:29–30)

The older son's words were filled with resentment toward his father and younger brother upon learning of his father's expensive celebration of the return of his younger irresponsible brother, who squandered his share of his father's wealth.

The Father's Explanation

Upon hearing the older son's complaint and his refusal to come in, the father did not demand that his aggrieved son ought to come into the house to tell him of his concerns. Instead, the father went out immediately to meet his aggrieved son; this is the father's gesture of concern for the dissenting son. Further, this action of the father implies, "Son, I owe you an explanation."

There are two parts to the father's explanation to the dissenting son. First, the father explained his actions in the context of the dissenting son's standing with him. The father said what was obvious and true about the older son: *"My son," the father said, "you are always with me, and everything I have is yours"* (Luke 15:31).

The father's response to the dissenting son implies, "I have not compromised what belongs to you." For the dissenting son to accept the above statement of his father as true, the father-leader should have a reputation for always telling the truth. A leader's honest explanation to a dissenter is likely to be accepted if the leader has a reputation for always being truthful.

The Father's Justification

First, the father explained the context to his son, as mentioned above. Second, the father said, *"It was fitting to celebrate and be glad, for this your brother was dead, and is alive; he was lost, and is found"* (Luke 15:32 ESV).

The father's use of the word "fitting" here means it was **the right thing for him to do**.

Because the father did the right thing, there was no need for him to apologize or to withdraw his decision to celebrate his younger son's repentance and his return home.

The parable demonstrates that doing the right thing is the best defense against dissent, because the leader can then confidently say to the aggrieved dissenter, "I did the right thing."

Dealing with Dissent

Dissent is a part of every leader's life. As a leader, you can confidently explain your decision to aggrieved dissenters if you have a reputation for always speaking the truth and always doing what is right.

Discuss from a Christian Leader's Perspective:

1. Have you dealt with dissent as a leader, or have you seen other leaders deal with dissent? How does that compare with the parable above?

2. The father in the parable did not expect any dissent from his faithful son. Would you have expected the faithful son's dissent? Why?

3. In the future, how would you deal with dissent differently as a leader or as a parent based on the above?

Jesus Is a Role Model for Leaders

Lesson

Gentile Leader or
Servant Leader?

Then the mother of Zebedee's sons came to Jesus with her sons and, kneeling down, asked a favor of him. "What is it you want?" he asked. She said, "Grant that one of these two sons of mine may sit at your right and the other at your left in your kingdom." (Matthew 20:20–21)

Leaders Are Tempted

Matthew 4:21 identifies the two Zebedee brothers as James and John. We do not know if this incident was entirely their mother's effort, or if the brothers sought their mother to be the spokesperson for this magnificent request, which did not at all go well with Jesus. Since there is no record of her sons dissuading their mother in public, mother and sons appear to be on the same page.

This incident serves as an example of the temptations of leaders fueled by their family members. A parent, a spouse, children, or other family members may pressure a leader to seek high honor and position because they might like to bask in the glory and honor associated with of one of their own.

When the remaining ten disciples heard about this encounter, *"they were indignant with the two brothers"* (verse 24). Thus, the failed attempt to secure high honor, position, and glory had an immediate cost for the brothers: they offended the other members of the team of disciples.

Gentile Leaders Are Not Servant Leaders

Jesus took this incident as an opportunity to teach His disciples the differences between a servant leader and someone who is NOT a servant leader; Jesus calls such a leader a "**Gentile leader**."

> *Jesus called them* [His disciples] *together and said, "You know that the rulers of the Gentiles lord it over them, and their high officials exercise authority over them. Not so with you. Instead, whoever wants to become great among you must be your servant, and whoever wants to be first must be your slave—just as the Son of Man did not come to be served, but to serve, and to give his life as a ransom for many."* (Matthew 20:25–28)

Jesus forbids the following behaviors associated with Gentile leaders that are contrary to his life on Earth, and the very spirit of servant leadership:

1. Lording over those entrusted to leaders,

2. Eagerly exercising authority over those entrusted to leaders,

3. Seeking to be served as a leader, and

4. Seeking to be elevated to a place of high or highest honor.

This list of behaviors condemned by Jesus is associated with the term "Gentile" leadership, which is not servant leadership. The temptation to fervently seek one or more items in the above list is very human and is the norm. It is easier than you think to fall for the items in this list. Consider how the two brothers, having been with Jesus and witnessed His leadership model from close quarters, nevertheless became a part of a public attempt to gain high honor, position, and glory in God's kingdom. Jesus seemed to be disappointed.

A servant leader has victories over the four items in the list above.

Jesus Is a Leader's Role Model

It is not surprising that Jesus told His disciples NOT to use Gentile leaders as a role model. Instead, Jesus offered Himself as the role model for a servant leader devoted to serving others. Jesus' agenda for leaders runs counter to the Gentile leaders' version above; His agenda is:

1. Be a servant and seek to serve others;

2. Humble yourself to a position that is as low as possible, even to the level of a slave; and

3. Be giving to others, just as Jesus went to the extreme to give away His life for others.

See the marked contrast between the two lists above: no overlap, and nothing in common. Therefore, when Gentile leaders serve as your role model, you will end up displacing Jesus from that role in your life.

To be a servant leader, you need many essential victories over the strong temptations to be a Gentile leader. As a servant leader, do you have those essential victories over the temptations to be a Gentile leader?

Discuss from a Christian Leader's Perspective:

1. What are the behaviors that are contrary to servant leadership according to Jesus Christ?

2. According to Jesus, how could you experience victory over the behaviors that are contrary to servant leadership?

3. What are your challenges for being a servant leader as defined by Jesus Christ?

LESSON 21

Jesus Deals with
Deceptive Enemies

A Devious Plot to Trip Jesus

Christian leaders do get tested or challenged by deceptive enemies;
they can learn from Jesus on how they may deal with such tests
and challenges. For example, certain men sent by the Pharisees
employed a deceptive setup to trap Jesus:

> *Then the Pharisees went out and laid plans to trap Jesus
> using His words. They sent their disciples to him along with
> some Herodians.*
>
> *"Teacher," they said, "we know that you are a man of integ-
> rity and that you teach the way of God in accordance with
> the truth. You aren't swayed by others, because you pay no
> attention to who they are. Tell us then, what is your opin-
> ion? Is it right to pay the imperial tax to Caesar or not?"*
>
> *Jesus, knowing their evil intent, said, "You hypocrites, why
> are you trying to trap me?"* (Matthew 22:15–18)

Those who posed the above question to Jesus intended to trap Him
in the presence of the Herodians, who were loyal to Herod and
had the imperial authority to collect taxes by force, if needed. The
questioners and those who sent them to Jesus had hoped that Jesus
would say something to the effect of "Don't pay imperial taxes to
Caesar," within earshot of the Herodians. This appears to be the
intended plot.

Incidentally, while these men DID NOT mean what they said to
Jesus during the setup, they spoke the truth about Jesus as part of

99

their deception—so pay attention to what they said. Here are four examples of what they said and what they likely believed:

1. They said, "Teacher, we know that you are a man of integrity." But they believed that Jesus was a false teacher. They did not trust Him as the Messiah, the Son of God, the fulfillment of the Scriptures, or the only way to God.

2. They said, "You teach the way of God in accordance with the truth." But they believed that His teachings were false and rubbish, and that He was NOT the one trained and disciplined to teach the truth.

3. They said, "You aren't swayed by others, because you pay no attention to who they are." But they were thinking, "We want to puff you up. You think you are not swayed by others including the Roman rulers, but we are smart enough to know how to trip you up and get you on the wrong side of the Roman rulers over imperial taxes that are due to Caesar."

4. They said, "What is your opinion?" This was a dishonest request. They had no intention of learning from Jesus, and they did not care for any of His opinions. They wanted to hear His opinion so He would fall into the hands of the Roman rulers. They expected His words to bring a swift rebuke, or worse, from the Roman authorities, as well as His public humiliation.

An Objective Response from Jesus

Not perturbed by what He heard and knowing their intent, Jesus went on to say,

> *"Show me the coin used for paying the tax." They brought him a denarius, and he asked them, "Whose image is this? And whose inscription?"*

"Caesar's," they replied.

Then he said to them, "So give back to Caesar what is Caesar's, and to God what is God's."

When they heard this, they were amazed. So they left him and went away." (Matthew 22:19–22)

It is notable that Jesus was NOT angry, emotional, or upset upon sensing the trap. Instead, He was very objective. He asked for visual evidence (i.e., a coin) to base His answers on. Thus, Jesus answered their question objectively using the coin, even though they were devious and dishonest.

Amazed, Defeated, and Unforgiven

It was a brilliant move by Jesus to ask them for a Roman coin and employ it as "Exhibit A" in His response. Jesus' response took the wind out of His enemies' sails; they must have sensed the defeat of their ploy to trip Him up!

Remember, Jesus also said to them, *"and* [give back] *to God what is God's."* They had the opportunity to do so. But did they?

The devious men, in their amazement, could have said, "Lord, You are the Son of God; glory to God," or something similar to Nathaniel's exclamation when he met Jesus: *"Rabbi, you are the Son of God; you are the king of Israel"* (John 1:49). Because praise and honor belong to God, these are examples of giving back to God what belongs to Him.

Further, the men could have given Jesus the chance to forgive them by confessing to their plot and pleading for His forgiveness before they went away. But alas, not one of them appears to have done so. Sadly, they left Jesus and went away defeated and unforgiven.

This passage shows how Christian leaders may remain objective when tested and challenged.

Discuss from a Christian Leader's Perspective:

1. Have you dealt with deception, or have you witnessed other leaders dealing with deception? How was it similar or different from the above?

2. Have you or any leader you know responded to deception with an emotional response? How did it turn out? What are the lessons from the episode?

3. When Jesus did not fall for their deception, and when He gave them a wise response, why do you think the men left without asking for His forgiveness?

Extraordinary Outcomes of Leaders Working with God

Lesson

A Future with or without God

That night all the members of the community raised their voices and wept aloud. All the Israelites grumbled against Moses and Aaron, and the whole assembly said to them, "If only we had died in Egypt! Or in this wilderness! Why is the LORD bringing us to this land only to let us fall by the sword? Our wives and children will be taken as plunder. Wouldn't it be better for us to go back to Egypt?" And they said to each other, "We should choose a leader and go back to Egypt." (Numbers 14:1–4)

Fear-Induced Rebellion

The above rebellion occurred when the team of scouts returned from Canaan and gave their report to Moses and the nation of Israel. The scouts presented a split decision to Moses and others. The majority of the scouts, ten out of twelve, were intimidated by what they saw in the Promised Land. They were against entering it because they were certain the nation of Israel would be overwhelmed and obliterated by the local residents and nations. The people swallowed this negative view, and the result was total fear and paranoia among the people.

The Majority Opinion Was Wrong

Ten of the twelve scouts said, *"'We can't attack those people; they are stronger than we are.' And they spread among the Israelites a bad report about the land they had explored"* (Numbers 13:31–32). However, a minority of scouts, Joshua and Caleb, disagreed with the majority of scouts and said:

> *"The land we passed through and explored is exceedingly good. If the Lord is pleased with us, he will lead us into that land, a land flowing with milk and honey, and will give it to us. Only do not rebel against the Lord."* (Numbers 14:7–9)

If you are looking for evidence that the majority is not always right, this is an outstanding example. Here, most of the scouts were wrong because they misread what was ahead of them, plunging the nation of Israel into a sea of fear and despair.

But a minority of just two of the scouts read the opposition right. The two who predicted their nation's success in the Land of Canaan would depend on God. They said, *"If the Lord is pleased with us, he will lead us into that land ... and will give it to us"* (vs. 8).

They saw their success in the Promised Land entirely as an act of God. The strength and the might of the locals did not figure in their calculation.

The Majority Opinion Left Out God's Role

In contrast, the majority left God out of their calculations. They based their entire assessment on the perceived size and might of the locals in the Promised Land. They were terrified.

Given that the nation of Israel was entirely made of former slaves under the Egyptians, they were not trained warriors and had no war-making equipment. Without God, they were justified in being terrified at the prospect of going to war against native armies in the Promised Land.

God's Role Changes Everything

Scouts Joshua and Caleb correctly realized the job of overcoming the trained and armed soldiers in the Promised Land belonged to the Lord.

The knee-jerk reaction of the nation of Israel was to flee back to Egypt out of fear of what was ahead in the Promised Land. Without God in their equation, fleeing to Egypt appeared to be a better option for them. They were prepared to go back to Egypt and serve as slaves once again; if they had, they might have found the Egyptians harsher as masters and slave drivers.

It is not a surprise that the people were despondent and depressed if they could not and did not see a role for God in their lives.

Remember What God Has Done for Us

Except for Moses, Aaron, Caleb, and Joshua, the people of the nation of Israel FORGOT that God brought them out of Egypt to the edge of the Promised Land while performing great signs along the way. God said to Moses, *"How long will they refuse to believe in me, in spite of all the signs I have performed among them?"* (Numbers 14:11).

This verse reveals what God expects from us—that is, to trust in Him because of all the things He has done in our lives. Therefore, we need to keep track of what God has done for us; God expects us to do so. Going forward, God expects us to remember and be thankful for what He has already done.

Because Moses remembered the history of what God had done for His people, at this point in history, he faced the future without fear, unlike the forgetful nation of Israel. This was a major reason why Moses was a great leader. The nation of Israel should have been grateful to God for choosing Moses as their leader; he was hand-picked by God (Exodus chapter 3).

In the matter of remembering God's work in your life, are you more like Moses or the nation of Israel?

Discuss from a Christian Leader's Perspective:

1. Have you witnessed fear-induced rebellion against God in your life or in others?

2. Have been in situations in which your opinion contradicted everyone else or most others? How did you handle the ensuing pressures or conflict?

3. What do you learn from Moses when everyone disagrees or rebels against you, the leader?

Work with Jesus for Impossible Outcomes

Compassionate Leader

When Jesus landed and saw a large crowd, he had compassion on them, because they were like sheep without a shepherd. So he began teaching them many things.

By this time it was late in the day, so his disciples came to him. "This is a remote place," they said, "and it's already very late. Send the people away so that they can go to the surrounding countryside and villages and buy themselves something to eat."

But he answered, "You give them something to eat."

They said to him, "That would take more than half a year's wages! Are we to go and spend that much on bread and give it to them to eat?"

"How many loaves do you have?" he asked. "Go and see."

When they found out, they said, "Five—and two fish."

Then Jesus directed them to have all the people sit down in groups on the green grass. So they sat down in groups of hundreds and fifties. Taking the five loaves and the two fish and looking up to heaven, he gave thanks and broke the loaves. Then he gave them to his disciples to distribute to the people. He also divided the two fish among them all. They all ate and were satisfied, and the disciples picked up twelve basketfuls of broken pieces of bread and fish. The number of the men who had eaten was five thousand. (Mark 6:34–44)

In the above passage, Jesus observed a problem or need: "They were like sheep without a shepherd." One of the qualities of a great leader is the ability to recognize a problem or need.

Upon recognizing the problem, Jesus responded with compassion. It is the quality of a leader's response to the need that sets a great leader apart from ordinary leaders. A compassionate leader is one who takes the opportunity to minister to those who are in need but are unable to help themselves. Jesus set an example here for His disciples.

The Disciples Followed Jesus' Lead

Later in the passage, the disciples recognized that it was time for a meal for the thousands of hungry people who had come to hear Jesus. So the disciples came to Jesus with a **practical solution**. The disciples demonstrated leadership when they noticed a need and responded with a solution, too.

We notice in the passage above that Jesus proposed a different solution to the disciples; instead of sending the crowd away to fetch their food from the towns nearby, which was the practical solution proposed by His disciples, Jesus instructed them to feed the crowd right then and there! This baffled the disciples. Their response to Jesus may be paraphrased, "You are asking us to do the impossible!"

In response, Jesus first directed His disciples to find out how many loaves of bread were available. The disciples must have wondered, "Why is the Lord asking us to find out how many loaves of bread are available? A few loaves of bread cannot feed thousands!" Yet they followed His instruction.

Next, Jesus directed His team of disciples to seat thousands of people on the grass in preparation for a meal. Although the disciples saw no evidence of enough food to distribute, we can assume they turned their attention to seating thousands of people to receive food and to eat in an orderly manner without confusion.

Jesus accepted the few loaves of bread and fish the disciples brought to Him, prayed and blessed the food, and gave it to His disciples to distribute. The task of distributing food to 5,000 men plus thousands of women and children must have been an enormous task for the disciples, but it appears that they successfully completed their task.

The disciples carried out the instructions of Jesus Christ that included: 1) locating and bringing a few loaves of bread and a few fish to Jesus Christ to bless; 2) seating thousands of men, women, and children on the grass; 3) distributing food to thousands in an orderly manner; and 4) gathering the leftover food.

The Impossible Becomes Possible

The Bible records many spontaneous miracles of Jesus Christ (walking on water, etc.), or miracles in response to pleas from suffering individuals (blind, sick, etc.) or family members. In contrast, in the above case, although the disciples had a practical solution for the problem/need, Jesus overruled their practical solution with a spontaneous miracle.

The disciples abandoned their own practical solution to work with Jesus on what they thought was an "impossible" solution: feeding the thousands then and there. In the process, the disciples participated in an extraordinary, miraculous outcome. They witnessed the "impossible" become "possible."

There is a lesson here for Christian leaders with a heart to serve others with compassion: They may participate in great outcomes, even miraculous ones, by working with Jesus when the "impossible" may become "possible."

Discuss from a Christian Leader's Perspective:

1. Does Jesus call Christian leaders to work with Him?

2. Could Jesus work with His disciples without their willing participation?

3. The disciples did not know what the outcome would be, but they did the needful and all that was asked of them to see Jesus carry out the impossible. Can you relate to this experience of Jesus' disciples?

How to Lead Your People to Jesus Christ

A Woman Meets Jesus by Chance

An incident is described in detail in John's Gospel (John 4:4–43), in which a weary Jesus met a local Samaritan woman when He sat down beside what was known as "Jacob's well" in Samaria. She is often identified as "the woman at the well":

> Now he had to go through Samaria. So he came to a town in Samaria called Sychar, near the plot of ground Jacob had given to his son Joseph. Jacob's well was there, and Jesus, tired as he was from the journey, sat down by the well. It was about noon.
>
> When a Samaritan woman came to draw water, Jesus said to her, "Will you give me a drink?" (His disciples had gone into the town to buy food.)
>
> The Samaritan woman said to him, "You are a Jew and I am a Samaritan woman. How can you ask me for a drink?" (For Jews do not associate with Samaritans.) (John 4:4–9)

She chose to have a conversation with Jesus with probing questions for Him. Based on His answers, she concluded, "Sir, I perceive you are a prophet" (verse 19). Later, during the conversation, when she said to Jesus, "I know that Messiah" (called Christ) "is coming. When he comes, he will explain everything to us," Jesus revealed to her that He was the Messiah (verses 25–26).

A Proactive Woman

> *Then, leaving her water jar, the woman went back to the town and said to the people, "Come, see a man who told me everything I ever did. Could this be the Messiah?" They came out of the town and made their way toward him.* (John 4:28–30)

> *Many of the Samaritans from that town believed in him because of the woman's testimony, "He told me everything I ever did." So when the Samaritans came to him, they urged him to stay with them, and he stayed two days. And because of his words many more became believers.*

> *They said to the woman, "**We no longer believe just because of what you said; now we have heard for ourselves, and we know that this man really is the Savior of the world.**"* (John 4:39–42)

Upon hearing Jesus' claim that He was the Messiah, she acted promptly on her own to go and bring her townspeople to meet and hear Jesus before He could leave—perhaps she left her water jug (verse 28) near Jesus to indicate she would be back, or perhaps she thought she could run faster back to town without the water jug in her hand.

Notable Accomplishments

1. She did not wait for anyone to tell her to fetch her townspeople and bring them to Jesus. Once she realized they needed to hear Him, she acted. Leaders act when they see a need.

2. She formulated a message about Jesus for her townspeople.

3. Her message drew people to Jesus Christ very effectively. Her townspeople believed her and made the trip to meet

Jesus. *"Many Samaritans from that town believed in him because of the woman's testimony"* (verse 39).

4. Upon leading her people to Jesus, she let Jesus do the rest. After hearing Jesus, they said to the woman, ***"It is no longer because of what you said that we believe, for we have heard for ourselves, and we know that this is indeed the Savior of the world"*** (verse 42).

The blessed meeting of her townspeople with Jesus Christ became a reality because of the prompt actions and message of the woman who met Jesus at the well. She earned the right to be called "the woman who **led her town to Jesus Christ**," instead of being labeled merely "the woman at the well."

A Lesson for Leaders

As leaders, we can learn this from her: Once you recognize an opportunity to enlarge God's Kingdom, act promptly. If you do, just like this woman, you too may experience the joy of bringing your entire "town" to meet Jesus Christ; let Jesus do the rest.

Discuss from a Christian Leader's Perspective:

1. The woman in this narrative actively engaged Jesus Christ in an extended conversation. It led her to believe in Jesus. How could you or your organization encourage non-believers to take active interest in knowing Jesus Christ?

2. What enabled the woman in this story to believe she could quickly convince the people of her town to come and meet Jesus on short notice?

3. Could you speculate as to what she might have said that was convincing to her townspeople to respond so promptly?

Jesus Said:

"Very truly I tell you, whoever believes in me will do the works I have been doing, and they will do even greater things than these, because I am going to the Father." (John 14:12)

CPSIA information can be obtained
at www.ICGtesting.com
Printed in the USA
BVHW071329211220
596070BV00001B/58